Halal Wealth

Invest
Without Compromising
Your Values

Farhan Khalid

Disclaimer: The views expressed in this book are the opinions of the author and are not meant as investment advice nor as *fatwa* (ruling based on Islamic law).

All Quran verse translations included in this book are based on *The Clear Quran* by Dr. Mustafa Khattab (Book of Signs Foundation, Copyright © 2016).

Learn more about the author or reach out at heyiwroteabook.com.

Coconut Juice Publishing Co.

Copyright © 2021 Farhan Khalid

All Rights Reserved.

ISBN: 979-8-745-40092-6

Table of Contents

	Preface	1
1	Housekeeping	5
2	To Invest, or Not to Invest	11
	Halal vs. Haram	17
3	Lock, Stocks, and Two Smoking Barrels	20
	Types of Stocks	27
	Risk	30
	Picking Stocks	33
	Apps	37
	Purification	40
	How to Begin Investing	42
4	Funds Can Be Fun	49
	Types of Funds	53
	Islamic Funds	56
	Robo-Advisors	59
5	Unconventional Wisdom	64
	Employee Stock Purchase Plans	65
	Sukuk	67
	Futures and Options	69
	Annuities	71
	Real Estate	72
	Venture Capital	78
	Precious Metals	81
	Foreign Exchange	83
	Cryptocurrency	86
	Non-Fungible Tokens	91
6	Desire to Retire	95
	Social Security	96
	Pensions and 401(k)s	98
	Individual Retirement Accounts	103
	401(k) Rollover	108
7	Famous Last Words	113
	Glossary	120

Preface

Back in 2016 I wrote a book called *Open the Door to a Wealthier Life*. It was basically everything I wish I knew when I started my adult life. I aimed to make it a holistic book about money management, investing, big ticket purchases, retirement planning, etc.

A lot has changed since 2016, so I felt compelled to roll out an update to my previous book. Some of the concepts I discussed in that book are timeless, in my humble opinion, such as having the right mindset and managing one's money properly, so I don't feel the need to rehash those. The world of investing is ever-evolving, though, hence the encore.

There are a couple of other things that compelled me to write another book encouraging *halal* (permissible) wealth. During the Great Pandemic of 2020, it bothered me that people selfishly hoarded goods with no regard for others who needed those items. It bugged me even more that some people not only hoarded goods, but took advantage of supply and demand to sell those items at exorbitant prices to other hapless folks. This is unethical, and not unlike ticket scalping. The purpose of retail stores is to purchase items for personal use and consumption. If someone wants to become an authorized reseller, they should enter into a contract with a distributor and do it legitimately. It concerns me to see people of our faith pursue wealth by nefarious means.

In the Quran we learn that Prophet Shuaib (AS) said to his tribe:

"O my people! Give full measure and weigh with justice. Do not defraud people of their property, nor go about spreading corruption in the land. What is left as a lawful gain by God is far better for you if you are truly believers. And I am not a keeper over you." [11:85-86]

There was also the GameStop stock fiasco of early 2021. Some people saw this as the little guy sticking it to the man, a modern-day David vs. Goliath. But I didn't really see either side as being in the right. It's bad enough that hedge funds short stocks (that is, sell stocks they don't actually own) and bet on a company's failure, but for others to manipulate the system is treading into murky territory. This is just my opinion, but I see day trading as a form of gambling. People should invest in companies whose products they believe in and whose financials and management seem sound.

Anyway, I decided to take a different approach with this book than the first one and hone in on investing to help fellow Muslims build a *halal* portfolio (i.e. collection of investments). This is for those who want to cut to the chase and start investing now. My goal is not to give you specific suggestions on where to invest your money, but to inform you of all the choices available and educate you on how they work. I'll also provide my analysis on why a certain investment is permissible or not. You can then choose the investments that best suit you.

A couple things I should note: All dollar amounts are stated in US currency, and any fees stated are subject to change but were the fees at time of publication. There's also a glossary in the back of the book for select English and Arabic terms.

Housekeeping

So you want to be wealthy, but want to do it the *halal* way? Good for you. While there's no guarantee you will actually get rich, not to mention everyone's definition of rich will vary, we live in an era of abundance.

There's no shortage of resources and opportunities out there. What's more, we have myriad choices these days for *halal* investments. Whether you're a beginner or a seasoned investor looking to make some positive changes to your portfolio, *insha'Allah* (God willing) you'll find this book useful.

Before we delve into investing, I would like to touch on mindset. For starters, let's remember that all *rizq* (sustenance) is provided by Allah (SWT). Whatever is meant for us, we will receive. And anything we have, Allah (SWT) can take away at any moment. Still, we have to tie our camel, so to speak. Our job is simply to ensure that our income is earned through *halal* means, that we put our money to work instead of hoarding it, and that we're content with what Allah (SWT) provides us with. That's it.

Islam is about moderation in everything we do, even when it comes to commendable acts like prayer and fasting, as our bodies have a right over us. The same thing applies to money matters.

"Do not be so tight-fisted, for you will be blameworthy; nor so open-handed, for you will end up in poverty. Surely your Lord gives abundant or limited provisions to whoever He wills. He is certainly All-Aware, All-Seeing of His servants." [17:29-30]

Let's also take a moment to talk about success. What exactly is success? Is it a certain profession or salary level? Is it having a big house and a fancy car? Maybe, maybe not. Success should be what brings you true happiness and contentment. If that means a small, humble home and ample time with your family, more power to you. Don't let society or, dare I say, your parents define success for you. Think long and hard about what success means to you. It doesn't have to be set in stone. It's okay for it to evolve. Once you have a pretty clear picture of what you want out of life, you can begin to define the goals and concrete steps required to achieve that life.

Since we don't know exactly what is destined for us, we should set goals and strive for what we want, assuming that what we want is Islamically permissible. We should make *dua* (prayer) to Allah (SWT) for His help in achieving our goals, while also making plans and taking the requisite actions. When we make *dua*, we should have faith that Allah (SWT) will fulfill our wishes, and we should be patient. Don't give up. Sometimes Allah (SWT) has something better in store for us than what we asked for, and sometimes what we ask for may inadvertently cause us harm and thus Allah (SWT) protects us from it. And Allah (SWT) knows best.

Further, we shouldn't become obsessive about money. It's a tool, not an end-all and be-all. It's certainly useful in this world, but not something we can take with us to the afterlife. At the same time, try not to covet the material possessions others have. Some people go into debt to be able to show off a nice house and cars. To be frank, nobody cares about the tag on your clothing or the badge on your car, so no need to impress others.

A reminder from the Quran to myself and others:

"Competition for more gains diverts you from God, until you end up in your graves. But no! You will soon come to know...Then, on that Day, you will definitely be questioned about your worldly pleasures." [102:1-8]

I would also recommend avoiding debt whenever possible. Some people take out large interest-based mortgages or lengthy car notes in order to portray a certain lifestyle. Some rack up debt on credit cards so they can have material goods now. Young people take out student loans to attend big-name schools or pursue careers that their parents chose for them.

According to the Federal Reserve Bank of New York, combined US household debt reached $14.56 *trillion* by the end of 2020. A large chunk of this is mortgages, but also includes auto and student loans, not to mention credit card debt. It is possible to obtain the aforementioned things without incurring debt if you're willing to be patient. Not to sound reproving, but I'd be remiss not to mention that *riba* (interest) is prohibited in the Quran.

"...God has permitted trading and forbidden interest...God has made interest fruitless and charity fruitful..." [2:275-276]

Okay, enough lecturing. Let's dive into investing.

To Invest, or Not to Invest

Why Invest?

Well, why not? Would you rather your money sit in the bank and collect dust? It's not doing much good there. We know from the Quran that hoarding is frowned upon in no uncertain terms.

"...Give good news of a painful torment to those who hoard gold and silver and do not spend it in God's cause." [9:34]

What's more, once you factor in inflation, money in the bank is actually *losing* value. Inflation is basically the overall increase in prices, and it's something that has a direct impact on consumers like you and me. Over the past decade, the inflation rate in the US has averaged roughly 1.7% per year. I remember as a kid I could get candy or a can of soda out of a vending machine for a couple of quarters; now it takes at least a buck. That's inflation at work.

By investing your money, you're putting it to work and growing it, typically while helping others grow their businesses. It's a win-win situation where greater value is being created. By growing your money, hopefully at a higher rate of return than inflation, you have more wealth. And the more wealth you have, the more you can do in life, whether it's saving for *Hajj* (pilgrimage to Mecca), paying for your kid's college tuition, traveling the world, or engaging in philanthropy.

Aside from growing in value, the other aspect of investing to keep in mind is the concept of compounding. This is when you earn money on top of the money already earned. Let me give you an example. Suppose you invest $100 and earn 10% after Year 1. Your investment is now worth $110. Assuming you leave it alone and it earns another 10% after Year 2, this time it's growing 10% on top of $110. That gives you $121. That may not sound like much, but get this – after 10 years of growth at 10% per year, your original $100 will have grown to $259.37!

If you're a spreadsheet nerd like me, you can use the Future Value formula as follows:

=FV(0.1,10,0,100,1)

This example can be translated as 10% return rate over 10 years with no additional payments and with a $100 initial investment. Alternatively, you can use an online investment calculator such as calculator.net/investment-calculator.html.

How Much Should I Invest?

The short answer: As much as you can.

The conservative answer: As much as you can afford to lose.

Naturally, investing is not without risk. You have to assess your risk tolerance and your timeline. You should go into investing with the knowledge that you *could* lose it all. There's no guarantee. At the same time, you can mitigate risk in a variety of ways. You can choose to invest in stocks for established companies with a long history (i.e. blue-chip stocks), invest in mutual funds where risk is essentially pooled, or invest in something low-risk/low-return like *sukuk* (the Islamic equivalent of a bond). If you don't know what any of these terms mean, don't worry; I'll cover them over the next few chapters.

Generally speaking, the younger you are, the more risk you can take with investing because you have a longer timeframe to smooth out trend lines and experience gains. For instance, you can put more money into growing companies or maybe even startups. As you get older, or if you're getting started at a later age, then perhaps a more conservative approach is appropriate where you invest in lower-risk assets; you won't see massive returns, but you also decrease your risk of losing money. You can always adjust your portfolio to shift from aggressive investments to conservative ones, or vice versa. This is called rebalancing your portfolio.

Before really getting into investing, I recommend having three-to-six months' worth of living expenses saved up. You also have to consider your other obligations. Evaluate your current net income (i.e. your take-home pay) and your monthly bills, and see how much you are saving each month on average. That'll give you an idea of how much you could invest. Also calculate what percentage of your monthly income that figure is (that is, monthly savings divided by monthly net income). If you can only invest 3-5%

of your income for now, that's fine. Everyone's situation is different. See if you can work your way to up 10%, and eventually 15% or more if possible. This figure would represent all investments, including short-term, high-liquidity items like stocks and long-term things like an IRA for retirement savings. Again, don't worry if you have no clue what these things mean. Read on.

Why Invest the Halal Way?

There are tons of ways to make money. There are plenty of schemes one can devise to squeeze money out of people, plenty of companies one can invest in, and plenty of interest-based investments. So why bother with *halal* or ethical investing?

Ultimately it's going to be a personal choice. I'm simply delivering a message, and my message is that this life is temporary. The material pleasures of this world are fleeting. If we pursue wealth by any means necessary for the sake of worldly enjoyment, is it going to be worth it in the end? Are you willing to risk your *akhirah* (life in the Hereafter) for the sake of temporary gain?

There's no *barakah* (blessings) in money earned through unethical means. *Halal* wealth is pure wealth, and you can enjoy it without a guilty conscience.

What's Halal and What's Haram?

That's my two cents, but it begs the question – what exactly is *halal* investing? In short, it's putting your money into financial assets that avoid anything that's *haram* (impermissible). This means not buying stocks in companies that produce products or services like alcohol, porn, insurance, or gambling venues. Some would go so far as to exclude anything that could cause harm to the planet or its people, such as a firearms company.

It also means not throwing money into interest-bearing investments like Treasury or corporate bonds, savings accounts, money market accounts, or certificates of deposit (CDs). Check out the glossary for a bit more detail on these bank products.

Another example would be real estate investments where you are directly or indirectly earning mortgage interest. In fact, you can't loan money to someone and ask them to pay you back principal *and* interest.

"O believers! Fear God, and give up outstanding interest if you are true believers…But if you repent, you may retain your principal. Do no wrong and you will not be wronged." [2:278]

Later in the book I'll get into some other things that are either not allowed or wander into debatable territory. And, of course, I'll expand on what *is* allowed, beginning with the next chapter.

Who makes these rules? Some rulings are crystal clear from the Quran and teachings of the Prophet Muhammad (SAW). For complex topics and factoring in the modern landscape, there are a few agencies that aim to interpret scripture and *Shariah* (Islamic law), including:

- Accounting and Auditing Organization for Islamic Financial Institutions (AAOIFI): Founded in 1991, based in Bahrain

- Islamic Financial Services Board (IFSB): Founded in 2002, based in Malaysia

Both organizations work to provide standards for Islamic finance in line with *Shariah*. Which one is better, and which one should you follow? Those questions could be as contentious as asking when the Islamic holiday *Eid* is, and if it should be based on moon-sighting or calculation. Honestly, following the rulings by either organization is better than none at all.

Since I'm not an Islamic scholar, I simply try to stick with what's black-and-white and avoid the gray areas. Once again, I don't think it's worth jeopardizing one's fate in the Hereafter for the sake of a little money in this life.

It was reported by Abu Qatadah (AS) that Prophet Muhammad (SAW) said: "Verily, you will never leave anything for the sake of Allah Almighty but that Allah will replace it with something better." [Ahmad]

Lock, Stocks, and Two Smoking Barrels

One of the most common, easy, and appealing ways to invest is by purchasing stocks. The stock market is an integral part of the US economy, and it has been sensationalized by popular media. Just to name a few movies: *Wall Street* (1987), *Boiler Room* (2000), and *The Wolf of Wall Street* (2013).

What is the Stock Market?

You may have images in your mind from movies of a pit where a bunch of highly animated men are shouting incoherently. Thanks to technology, it's not quite like this nowadays, although it used to be.

Like any product or service, stocks require a marketplace where they can be traded, meaning bought and sold. The stock market isn't a physical store you go to for buying or selling shares of stock, nor is it a single website. You can access the stock market through a number of websites and apps, though, as well as through brick-and-mortar brokerages if you're old-fashioned.

The stock market consists of exchanges. Exchanges are like stores, and these stores make up the entire marketplace. Just like different stores sell different products, different exchanges list different companies' stocks.

The two primary exchanges in the US are the New York Stock Exchange (NYSE) and Nasdaq (the artist formerly known as NASDAQ). These also happen to be the largest exchanges in the world based on market cap, which is calculated as **(Number of Shares Outstanding x Current Share Price)**. Exchanges have been around in the US for over two centuries. Other large exchanges include Shanghai Stock Exchange, Japan Exchange Group, London Stock Exchange, and TMX Group in Toronto.

What Are Stocks?

A stock can be thought of as a tiny piece of a company. It's a small portion of ownership or equity in the company. But not any old company. Stocks apply to corporations. For our purposes, let's focus on publicly traded corporations, as stocks sold by privately held corporations are a whole different ball game.

In any case, companies need to raise capital in order to build and grow their businesses, and one way to do this is by selling shares of stock. The company receives money from interested investors, which it can then put towards capital expenditures, research & development, marketing, etc.

If the company utilizes the money wisely and its products are selling well, investors benefit by seeing increased value in their shares of stock. If the company goes belly up, then investors lose the funds they invested. Investors only win if the company is winning (well, at least that's how it's supposed to work).

Assuming the company's stock price continues moving upward, investors can sell their stock for a higher price than what they paid and enjoy what's called a capital gain, or simply hold onto the stock for as long as they wish. Some companies (typically more established companies) even pay out dividends, which are small payments the company gives back to investors out of its profits. Dividends are sort of a reward or thanks for investors, but also benefit the company by enhancing its image and goodwill.

Companies only issue a finite number of shares to the marketplace. As for how stock prices are determined, good old supply and demand is a big part of it, but there's more to it. If the company is about to launch a new product, that could get investors interested enough to scoop up stocks and reduce supply, thereby increasing demand for what's left. Companies may also buy back their own shares, which too can have the effect of reducing supply while driving up price on the remaining shares. But a company's valuation will also increase if the company is doing well and its financial metrics reflect that.

To give you an example, suppose you buy 100 shares of stock in the fictitious company Decadent Desi Desserts Inc. at $10/share shortly after the company launches. At this point, you've invested $1,000. Five years later, business is booming, having catered for many large Indian weddings with Instagram-worthy, rainbow spreads of mouth-watering sweets. Stocks are now valued on the market at $20 apiece. That's double the value of when you first invested! If you like, you could now sell all 100 shares for $2,000, leaving you with a capital gain of a whopping $1,000.

Now You've Got My Attention – Tell Me More

When a corporation first decides to go public, an Initial Public Offering (IPO) takes place. Plenty of due diligence takes place before such a big move, and there can be a lot of hype that increases demand for the stock before it even goes live. After the IPO, the company's stock is continuously traded on the stock market. This latter activity is known as the secondary market, whereas the IPO is done on the primary market.

Stocks are identified by ticker symbols, which are abbreviations. In the US, ticker symbols usually consist of one to four letters, although other countries use different formats. A few examples of companies traded publicly in the US are AAPL for Apple, AMZN for Amazon, FB for Facebook, and TSLA for Tesla.

One of the advantages of owning stock is that it's considered a liquid investment. That is, if you need cash right now, you can sell some stock and have the funds transferred from your brokerage account to your bank account. Something like real estate is considered illiquid because the whole process to sell a property and acquire the funds takes considerably longer.

Speaking of cash, I recommend using only your own cash in order to buy stocks. "How else would I buy stocks," you ask? There's something called margin, where you can borrow money from a brokerage to buy stocks. It's a loan, and an interest-bearing one at that. If you buy using margin and end up making a poor investment choice, you're still responsible for paying back the loan. I see trading on margin as no different than a gambler borrowing money from a loan shark. Those situations don't always end well.

How Does a Company Get Onto the Stock Market?

It's not as easy as placing one's products for sale on eBay or Etsy. Assuming a business is already incorporated, it must go through a process in order to become "public". In the US, the company must file a form with the Securities and Exchange Commission (SEC), a regulatory body. The company must also pen a prospectus, a document that describes the business and includes details on its financials.

The company also has to decide which exchange it wants to be listed on (i.e. NYSE or Nasdaq), and comply with that exchange's requirements. It also gets to choose a ticker symbol. There will be underwriters and lawyers involved, and additional paperwork. Once it's all said and done, the company can finally proceed with an IPO.

Are All Stocks Created Equal?

There are two main types of stocks: common and preferred.

Common stocks are pretty common, as you probably deduced by the name. The bulk of stocks sold on the stock market are considered common. Some people prefer preferred stocks because there's normally a guaranteed dividend of a fixed amount. Common stocks may or may not offer dividends, and the amount will vary even if a dividend is paid out. I should point out, however, that some scholars see fixed dividends as equivalent to interest payments, making preferred stocks gray area at best, *haram* at worst.

By the way, since we're on the topic of dividends, I should note that dividends are considered a form of income. Each year you'll receive a 1099-DIV form detailing dividend income, and you'll have to input these figures when you file taxes, or provide the form to your tax preparer.

There are some other differences between common and preferred stock. Shareholders of common stock have voting rights, while shareholders of preferred stock do not. Voting takes place during the company's annual meeting, and the more shares of common stock a person owns, the greater his/her number of votes.

Also, if a company goes bankrupt, there will be a whole line of people trying to get money out of the company, namely creditors. Preferred shareholders may be able to recoup some or all of their investment, while common shareholders will likely recoup nothing. To spot preferred stocks on an exchange, look for "P" at the end of the ticker symbol or some reference to "preferred" or "pfd".

Aside from common and preferred stocks, companies can choose to offer different classes of stocks with different rights or benefits. You may see something like Class A, B, and C being offered. A classic example is investing guru Warren Buffett's Berkshire Hathaway stock. Class A's ticker symbol is BRK-A and costs way, way, way more per share than the Class B version BRK-B. What do you get for the price premium of the former version? More voting rights.

We can further categorize stocks based on what they offer to investors. Examples include: blue-chips for well-established firms, as mentioned earlier; income stocks that pay steady dividends; value stocks, which may take years to grow in value but have plenty of potential; and growth stocks, which are up-and-coming and can experience big gains (but possibly big losses as well).

There's also another type of stock called penny stocks, which are cheap common stocks (could be less than a dollar per share) for questionable companies. Not to say that all penny stocks are bad, but I'd rather stick with reputable companies and not bother with these. If someone urged me to buy a particular penny stock, I'd have to question their motive.

Isn't Buying Stocks Risky?

It's natural to worry about the ups and downs of the market, but that's like anything in life. If you're day trading, sure, there's going to be risk. If you want the stress and heartache associated with ogling your stock portfolio everyday, it's up to you, but I take a set-it-and-forget-it approach. I'm more concerned with long-term value.

If you look at historical figures for the Dow Jones Industrial Average (DJIA) over the course of a century, you can clearly see that the historical trend is upwards. The following chart displays data from February 1915 to February 2021.

Source: https://www.macrotrends.net/1319/dow-jones-100-year-historical-chart

If you view a stock chart for one day or five days of data, it can appear startling. But that view is rather myopic. If you step back and look at the one-year or five-year history of that stock, you'll get a totally different picture. Keep in mind that the historical, average rate of return on the stock market is 7-8% after factoring in inflation. Not too shabby. Sometimes you have to zoom out to get the whole picture.

Furthermore, you can mitigate risk by diversifying your portfolio. This means purchasing stocks in a variety of companies from different industries. That way, even if one company goes south, the overall value of your portfolio won't take a huge hit.

In general, smaller companies are more susceptible to volatility, but on the plus side they have potential for greater growth. Big companies that have been around for a long time might not see massive growth, but are typically more stable in their stock prices. A mix of stocks in small, medium, and large companies from different industries can lead to a well-diversified portfolio. An easy way to diversify is by buying a fund, which I'll expand on in the next chapter, but a fund is essentially a collection of stocks.

Don't put all your eggs into one basket if you're risk-averse. Additionally, evaluate each company whose stock you want to buy and make an informed decision based on the company's merits and financial stability.

There's also the risk and reward factor. If you take higher risks, there's a possibility (but no guarantee) of higher returns. Nothing wrong with taking a more conservative approach, though. Based on your expendable income, proximity to retirement, and risk tolerance, you can decide which approach is best for you.

Investing is like chess. You have to have patience and discipline. In the investing world, bearish investors worry about prices going down and may even sell investments at a loss before they drop further in value. Bullish investors, on the other hand, are more optimistic and believe prices will go up.

Is it better to be a bull than a bear? Not necessarily, and not if you work in a china shop, but I'd rather be a bull. Either way, don't let the ups and downs of the market worry you too much. The economy and the stock market will always have fluctuations, but to panic due to short-term lulls is unhealthy. Think long-term.

How Do I Choose Stocks?

If only it were as easy as picking companies you like. When it comes to choosing stocks that are in line with Islamic values, there are three main factors to consider: the company's core business, how leveraged the company is, and how liquid the company is.

Core business refers to what a company produces or performs in order to make money. Obviously, any company a Muslim invests in should not be involved in offering *haram* products or services such as alcohol, interest-bearing products, pornography, pork products, or gambling. Some scholars advise not to invest in companies that produce harmful products, such as weapons or cigarettes.

The exception to the rule is that if a company's core business is *halal* but it earns less than 5% of its revenue through something *haram*, it's still considered acceptable to invest in. However, you would then be required to purify your investments. I'll explain how to do this shortly.

Leverage refers to how much debt a company has. A highly leveraged company has taken out a high dollar amount worth of loans. It owes a lot of money to creditors. To be *Shariah*-compliant, the total debt can be only one-third (33.33%) or less of its market cap. Debt can be found on a financial statement called the balance sheet using Yahoo! Finance (finance.yahoo.com) or a similar site. The calculation for leverage is:

(Total Liabilities) / (Number of Shares Outstanding x Current Share Price)

Liquidity refers to how much money a company holds in the form of cash, cash equivalents, and accounts receivable (i.e. money owed to the company by its customers for products sold or services performed). These figures can be found on a company's balance sheet. Once you have this sum, you can compare it to the total assets, a figure that will also be listed on the balance sheet. To be acceptable, liquidity should be no higher than 45%. The calculation is as follows:

(Cash + Cash Equivalents + Net Receivables) / Total Assets

Aside from these calculations to determine if a stock is *Shariah*-compliant, you should also review the company's financials in general to see how it's performing. Also look up news about the company to gauge not only how it's doing now, but to make an educated guess on how it's going to do going forward.

One metric worth looking at is Earnings Per Share (EPS), which gives an indication of a company's profitability. You can find EPS on a stock's profile page. The higher it is the better, although EPS can be misleading because it can be skewed if a company has fewer number of shares outstanding.

A calculation you can do using figures from the income statement is **(Net Income / Total Sales Revenue)**. This will give you Net Profit Margin. If it's 10% or higher, it indicates the company is doing a good job of keeping expenses under control.

Another metric is Current Ratio, which is calculated as **(Current Assets / Current Liabilities)**. Check out the company's balance sheet for these figures. Current Ratio gives you an idea of how easily a company can pay its bills. A healthy range is 1.5 to 2.0. If it's below 1, that's not a good sign, although it's not the whole story, either.

One last metric I'll mention is Beta. You can find this figure listed on Yahoo! Finance or other sites with stock info. Beta is a measurement of how volatile a stock is, potentially, relative to the stock market in general. If it's lower than 1, the stock should be less volatile, while higher than 1 indicates greater volatility.

Isn't There An Easier Way?

Why yes, there is. If crunching numbers isn't your thing, you can take advantage of technology to do the heavy lifting for you.

One excellent app to download is Zoya, available for iOS and Android devices. After downloading it and logging in, you can see a listing of companies by industry, or search by company name or ticker symbol. You can even add companies to a watchlist, as *Shariah*-compliance can change over time as a business evolves. After selecting a company, you'll see its current stock price along with a chart, compliance status, key stats, and related news stories. This is all with the free version. With the paid version of the app, you get additional features like in-depth analysis and email alerts.

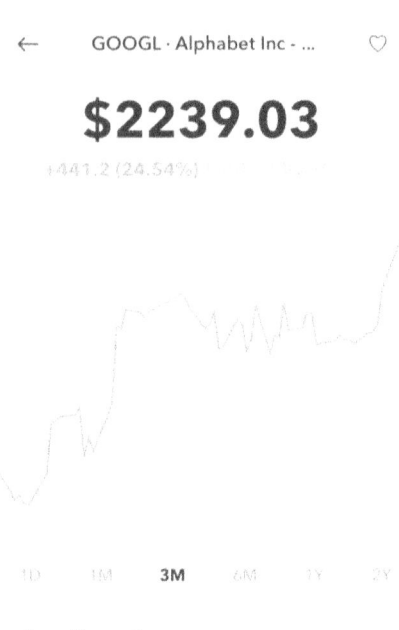

Another tool is Finispia, which you can access via web browser at app.finispia.com. After logging in, you can search by company name or ticker symbol. Like Zoya, you'll get current stock price along with a chart and key stats. The interesting thing about Finispia, though, is that it shows *Shariah*-compliance according to five different standards. That way you can be more discerning and make an informed decision about whether or not to buy that stock. If the stock failed according to one of the standards, you can find out why by clicking on the Fail icon. One thing worth noting is that the free version only allows you to search for three stocks per month. If you're a pretty active trader, you'll want to opt for one of the paid subscription plans.

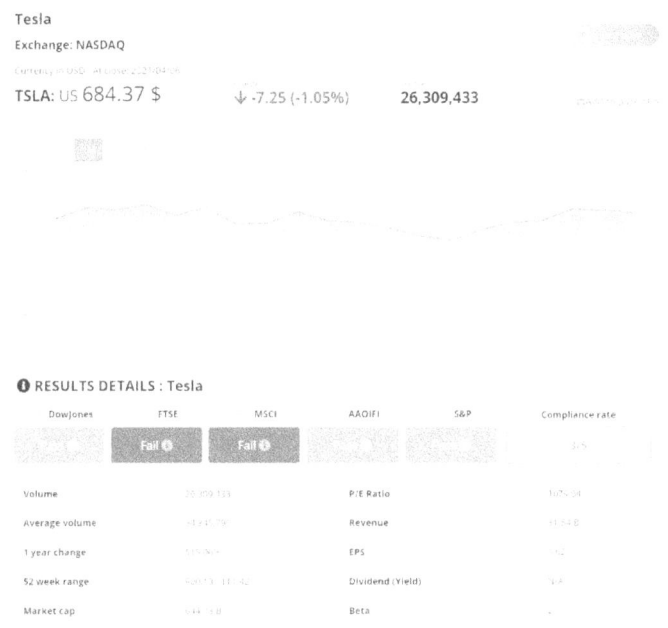

In early 2021 a new website launched called Halal Investors (halalinvestors.com) on which a couple of people provide their opinion on whether or not a company would be okay to invest in. They provide their comfort level, but it's not meant to be a definitive ruling on *Shariah*-compliance.

How Do I Purify My Investments?

If you've invested in stocks or funds that are technically compliant but the companies happen to earn a small amount of revenue through *haram* means, you must purify your investments. According to AAOIFI standards, you should perform the following calculation to determine the purification amount:

(Total Non-Compliant Revenue / Total Outstanding Shares) x (Number of Shares Held)

Once you determine the purification amount, you can donate that amount to a charity of your choice. You can find total outstanding shares through a simple Google search such as "AAPL outstanding shares". Figuring out non-compliant revenue is a little trickier, though.

Another option is to use an app like Islamicly, which is available for iOS and Android devices. You can also use it via web browser at islamicly.com. Its calculation is slightly different, as it uses **(Total Non-Permissible Revenue / Total Revenue)** to determine a Dividend Purification Ratio. Details of what goes into the calculation can be found at blog.islamicly.com/purification-of-shariah-compliant-stocks. With the app, you can select a stock tile and hit Purify, then enter the value of dividends received and it will calculate the purification amount for you. Just a side note, Islamicly sends a lot of emails if you sign up with them.

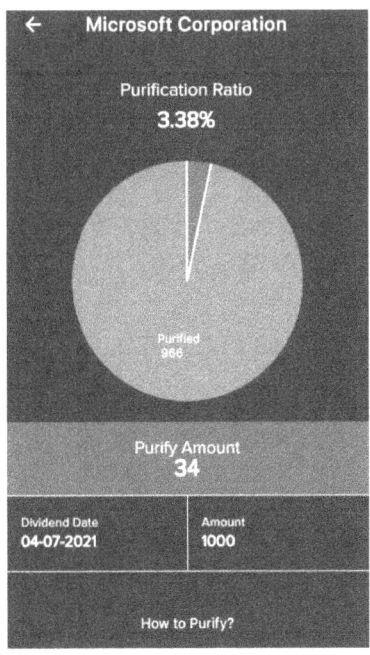

Where Do I Sign Up?

Alright, so now you're sold on investing in stocks. You know how the system works, and you know how to pick *Shariah*-compliant stocks. What next?

You need a platform through which you can access the stock market to actually buy and sell stocks. You could hire the services of a traditional stock broker, or you could sign up for a service like ShariaPortfolio (shariaportfolio.com) where you get a personal financial advisor and a customized portfolio. ShariaPortfolio's Access service is only available for folks with a cool $100,000 of cash handy. A 100 Grand candy bar won't suffice.

In my opinion, the easiest way to buy stocks is to sign up with an online brokerage. There are many available. When I wrote my first book, most of the big players charged a commission fee for each trade, but the Robinhood app was a game-changer, as it began life as a commission-free app that aimed to make investing accessible to everyone. But when something claims to be totally free, I tend to be somewhat wary or at least cognizant of the fact that my personal data will be used and sold.

Rather than give a specific suggestion on which service to use, I'll mention several platforms that are available with a short description. At the end of the day, they pretty much offer the same thing.

- Robinhood (robinhood.com): New kid on the block; mobile app w/ modern interface; easy to use; commission-free trades for stocks and exchange-traded funds; no account minimum; offers fractional shares, meaning you can buy a portion of one stock ($1 minimum) that has a high share price
- Webull (webull.com): Newer company; headquartered in New York, but owned by a Chinese firm; mobile app or web browser; decent interface with built-in analytics tools; commission-free trades for stocks and exchange-traded funds; no account minimum
- M1 Finance (m1finance.com): Another newcomer; note that M1 uses a different model for trading where you pick the

percentage of your portfolio that you want to allocate to different stocks, rather than buying individual shares; commission-free trades for stocks and exchange-traded funds, but also has a paid service called M1 Plus; $100 account minimum; offers fractional shares; also offers some automation, such as automatic contribution
- E*Trade (etrade.com): The original online trading platform; mobile app or web browser; somewhat old-fashioned interface; commission-free trades for stocks and exchange-traded funds; no account minimum
- TD Ameritrade (tdameritrade.com): Acquired by Charles Schwab; mobile app or web browser; somewhat old-fashioned interface; commission-free trades for stocks and exchange-traded funds; no account minimum
- Charles Schwab (schwab.com): Older company; mobile app or web browser; somewhat old-fashioned interface; commission-free trades for stocks and exchange-traded funds; no account minimum; offers stock slices, meaning

you can buy a portion of one stock ($5 minimum) that has a high share price, but only for stocks in the S&P 500
- Merrill Edge (merrilledge.com): Owned by Bank of America; mobile app or web browser; somewhat old-fashioned interface; commission-free trades for stocks and exchange-traded funds; no account minimum

This is by no means an exhaustive list. The first few on the list are newer, smaller companies and may not offer the same level of customer service as the older, more established companies. On the other hand, the newer, smaller companies tend to do a better job when it comes to user interface/user experience (UI/UX) in their apps.

Another note: At the time of writing, TD Ameritrade and Charles Schwab each offer their own trading platforms. By the time you read this, perhaps the platforms (or at least certain features) will be merged into one. Time will tell. Who knows what other changes will have taken place by the time your eyes reach this page. In my first book, I mentioned OptionsHouse and TradeKing; these companies have since been acquired by E*Trade and Ally Invest, respectively.

To use any of these services, either download the app or go to their website and open an individual brokerage account. Opening an account will require providing personal information like social security number (for tax purposes) and some form of ID, so be ready for that. You will also need to add funds to the account before you can trade, typically by linking your bank account.

By the way, people outside of the US can also sign up with these services and buy stocks in US companies, as US law does not prohibit non-citizens/non-residents from owning US stock. Just be prepared to present the requisite documentation like passport or foreign tax ID.

Once you're registered, logged in, and have funds ready to go, I'd recommend searching the site or app for a tutorial video on getting started, although most modern sites and apps are easy enough to figure out by clicking around. When it comes to buying stock, there are a few methods. At first this may seem complex or intimidating, but ultimately it gives more control to the investor. Here's a quick overview of the common methods:

- Market: If you place a market order, the online brokerage will attempt to execute the purchase immediately at the current stock price.
- Market on Close: You place the order now, but it will execute at the closing share price when the market is about to close for the day.
- Limit: You set a limit price, meaning the highest price you're willing to pay per share. The purchase will only take place if the share price falls to that price or lower. Otherwise, the order will expire based on the duration you indicate. An example would be a stock currently trading at $50/share but that you're only willing to pay $48/share for.
- Stop: Like a limit order, you specify the highest price you're willing to pay, but this time it'll be higher than the market price. An example would be a stock trading at $65/share that seems to be steadily increasing, so you place a stop

order for $67/share. The order will then execute at $67, but hopefully the stock price will continue to rise.

Funds Can Be Fun

This chapter will be shorter than the former, as I already covered the fundamentals of stocks and much of that knowledge will apply here.

How Are Funds Different Than Stocks?

I know I mentioned mutual funds and exchange-traded funds (ETFs) in previous chapters, but I purposely didn't expand on them because I was waiting for this chapter. In this context, funds are not referring to money, but to a collection of stocks put together by an investing firm.

After putting together this bundle, they get investors to put money into the fund. All of that money is pooled and the fund manager invests it into the individual stocks. The investment firm will manage the fund, so it's hands-off and hassle-free for the individual investors.

Are Funds Right for Me?

For those who don't want the hassle of picking and choosing individual stocks and managing their portfolio, funds can be an excellent choice. Aside from making investing easier, funds also reduce risk because a single fund will contain many stocks. The number varies, but a typical fund will contain stocks for tens of different companies, and could easily contain over 100 different stocks.

If you're looking for ease and instant diversification, keep funds in mind. I should mention, however, that there is a small fee for having an investment firm manage a fund on your behalf. This is known as the expense ratio. As a simple example, suppose you put $1,000 into a mutual fund and that the fund's expense ratio is 1%. If the fund earned a return over the year of 10%, that would bring the value to $1,100. The fund will deduct 1% from that, or $11, leaving you with $1,089. This is something to be aware of if you're looking to maximize returns.

Aside from the expense ratio, there are a couple of other potential fees. There could be an early redemption fee. For example, the fund may state that if you withdraw in the first 90 days, they will charge a $50 fee. If the fund is classified as a load fund, there will be a small fee either when you buy the fund (i.e. front-end load) or sell the fund (i.e. back-end load). No-load funds do not charge such a fee.

Funds can be actively managed or passively managed. You can probably guess what they mean, but actively managed funds are just that. The fund manager actively reviews the fund's holdings and adjusts things as he/she sees fit. Because of the extra work involved, these tend to have higher expense ratios. Passively managed funds take more of a set-it-and-forget-it approach, and therefore have lower expenses associated with them. One might think an actively managed fund earns better returns because there's always a set of eyes on it, but the data suggests otherwise. Passively managed funds can perform quite well.

If you'd rather build your own custom portfolio with stocks of your choice, I'll share a little trick with you. If you do a Google search for "[fund name] holdings", you'll be able to pull up a list of all stocks that make up a fund. That could give you ideas for companies to invest in separately. Assuming you're searching for an Islamic fund, you can be reasonably sure that the companies listed have already been vetted for *Shariah*-compliance.

Different Flavors of Funds

There are a few types of funds. Mutual funds have been around for decades. Investment companies will put together a package of stocks and get investors to sign up and pool resources. They provide diversification and economies of scale. Mutual funds can be managed by larger, well-known companies like Vanguard or by lesser-known firms. To purchase a mutual fund, the investor fills out an application directly with that firm.

A modern spin on mutual funds is exchange-traded funds, or ETFs. These are essentially mutual funds that you can buy directly on the stock market with a per-share price. ETFs can be bought and sold throughout the day like stocks, and the per-share price can fluctuate as the day goes on just like stocks. If you already have a brokerage account, this can be an easy gateway into funds without having to sign up separately with another company. Some mutual funds are available in exchange-traded form, while some funds are exclusively exchange-traded and not available through traditional means.

There are also index funds, which can be either mutual funds or ETFs. These are passively managed funds designed to mimic the behavior of a popular index like the S&P 500, Nasdaq Composite, or Dow Jones Industrial Average (DJIA).

This is a good time to explain what indexes are. Indexes are also collections of stocks, but these aren't funds you invest in. They're hypothetical. These "portfolios" contain a segment of the total available stocks (i.e. 500 different companies in the S&P 500) and are designed to be representative of the market as a whole and indicative of how the market is doing. If you hear on the news that the S&P 500 is up today, that gives you a general sense that the stock market as a whole is doing pretty well. You can think of index funds as benchmarking a particular index.

Interestingly, there are various Islamic indexes available that track performance of *Shariah*-compliant stocks. One is the Dow Jones Islamic

Market World Index (DJIM). In the UK, the Financial Times Stock Exchange (FTSE) has a few indexes, such as FTSE Global Equity Shariah Index Series and FTSE Nasdaq Dubai Shariah Index Series. In Canada, S&P offers the TSX 60 Shariah Index.

Aside from the different fund types, there are also what I call styles of funds, based on the objective of the fund. For instance, growth funds invest in small or midsize companies that are still growing, which may have more risk but possibly more reward. Income funds invest in large, established, dividend-paying firms that can be safe, stable investment choices. International funds invest in emerging markets, which can be volatile but may have good growth potential in the future. There are also sector funds that hone in on a particular industry such as healthcare or technology and only invest in those types of stocks. A fund can, of course, be hybrid and contain aspects of each of these styles.

Well, Are There Islamic Funds?

There sure are. The veterans in this space include Amana Funds, Iman Fund, and Azzad Funds.

Amana (saturna.com) has the Income Fund, which focuses on steady, stable growth and dividends; the Growth Fund, which focuses on long-term value and growing companies; the Developing World Fund, which invests in companies in emerging markets outside of the US; and the Participation Fund, which aims to preserve capital by investing in *sukuk* (which I'll explain in the next chapter).

The Iman Fund (investaaa.com) offers just one fund, its namesake. This fund focuses on capital growth, rather than dividend income or capital preservation. I would say it most resembles the Growth Fund from Amana's lineup.

Azzad (azzadasset.com) offers two choices. The Ethical Fund is similar to the Iman Fund in that it invests in growing companies. The aim is long-term value rather than dividend income or capital preservation. The Wise Capital Fund is sort of like a combination of Amana's Income and Participation Funds in that it focuses on dividend income as well as capital preservation (with a bias towards the latter).

The newer players in the fund game include Wahed and ShariaPortfolio, both founded on Islamic principles to cater to Muslim investors. Wealthsimple is a Canadian company that offers an online investment platform as well as socially responsible investment funds, but not all of their offerings are *Shariah*-compliant. Likewise, there's an American investment firm called BlackRock that happens to offer a couple of *Shariah*-compliant funds for UK investors among other non-compliant products: iShares MSCI USA Islamic ETF and iShares MSCI World Islamic ETF.

Wahed (wahedinvest.com) offers one ETF, which went live in July 2019. It's called Wahed FTSE USA Shariah ETF, and is a passively managed index fund that aligns with the FTSE Shariah USA Index. It's a hybrid of growth and income. They have the perfect ticker symbol, too: HLAL.

ShariaPortfolio (sp-funds.com) has three offerings. Their first fund launched in 2019 and is called SP Funds S&P 500 Sharia Industry Exclusions ETF (SPUS). It's a growth-focused index fund that tracks the S&P 500 Sharia Industry Exclusions Index. Shortly after launching SPUS, their *sukuk*-based fund went live, called SP Funds Dow Jones Global Sukuk ETF (SPSK), offering a relatively safe and stable place to store money. Their latest offering is SP Funds S&P Global REIT Sharia ETF (SPRE), which is exciting because it focuses on real estate, or what are known as real estate investment trusts (REITs). This is a nice way to diversify one's portfolio to include real estate without the cost and hassle of owning and managing physical properties.

Wealthsimple (wealthsimple.com) is working on a fund for Canadian investors to be traded on the Toronto Stock Exchange called the Wealthsimple Shariah World Equity Index ETF (WSHR). It didn't launch at time of writing, but it will be a passively managed fund that tracks the Dow Jones Islamic Market Developed Markets Quality and Low Volatility Index. The fund will invest in stocks for companies in various sectors and aims for long-term growth.

BlackRock's iShares (ishares.com) MSCI USA Islamic ETF (ISUS) launched at the end of 2007 and trades on the London Stock Exchange. As you can tell from the fund's name, it invests in a variety of US companies and tracks the MSCI USA Islamic Index. The iShares MSCI World Islamic ETF (ISWD), on the other hand, invests in companies throughout the world and tracks the MSCI World Islamic Index. For your awareness, BlackRock has had some harassment and discrimination claims made against it by former employees.

The Robots Are Coming

Investing and devising a portfolio that's just right for you can take a lot of work. Thankfully, technology has caught up and there are now plenty of robo-advisors available to help investors build their portfolios. Unfortunately only a couple of these cater to Muslims.

The way a robo-advisor works is that the investor provides some input like his/her time horizon and aversion to risk. The robot then runs some algorithms and spits out the ideal investment mix.

When Wahed came onto the scene, it was a game-changer because it did what other robo-advisors did not. It filtered out certain industries like gambling and alcohol, as well as interest-based investments like conventional bonds. After signing up and taking a quiz, it will determine the appropriate risk level for the investor. You can also retake the quiz later if you want to adjust things. If you go to wahedinvest.com/portfolio, you can actually see a simulation of the risk levels and how the portfolio adjusts accordingly. For example, the more conservative you get, the more it will allocate funds to *sukuk* and less to equities (i.e. stocks).

Wahed will split up investment money between its own ETF, *sukuk*, gold, and cash. It has a minimum deposit of only $100, making it pretty accessible and easy for someone who's just getting started. Using a service like Wahed isn't free. They charge .79% annually if you have less than $100,000 in the account, and .49% if you have $100,000 or more. For example, if you have $10,000 in your Wahed account, they will take $79.

Another option is ShariaPortfolio Express. It's similar to Wahed in that it requires you to complete a questionnaire, and it will then provide an ideal portfolio breakdown between equities, *sukuk*, and cash. ShariaPortfolio Express has a $1,000 minimum. Their fees are .50% annually if you have less than $25,000 in the account, and .75% if you have $25,000 or more.

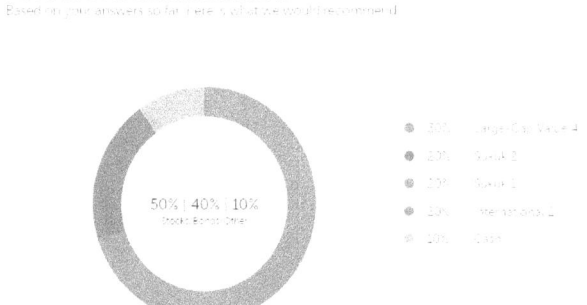

Table of Funds

For quick reference, following are a couple of tables listing the funds mentioned to help you decide which one is right for you. Note: The figures stated are subject to change, but this is what they were at time of writing.

Mutual Funds:

Fund Name	Ticker Symbol	Expense Ratio	Minimum Investment	Style
Amana Income	AMANX	1.04%	$250	Income
Amana Growth	AMAGX	0.99%	$250	Growth
Amana Developing World	AMDWX	1.34%	$250	Growth
Amana Participation	AMAPX	0.88%	$5,000	Capital Preservation
Iman	IMANX	1.33%	$250	Growth
Azzad Ethical	ADJEX	0.99%	$1,000	Growth
Azzad Wise Capital	WISEX	1.29%	$4,000	Income + Capital Preservation

To invest in any of these mutual funds, go to the fund's website and fill out the application. These funds are all no-load funds, meaning there's no commission fee for selling.

Exchange-Traded Funds:

Fund Name	Ticker Symbol	Expense Ratio	Style
Wahed	HLAL	0.50%	Growth + Income
ShariaPortfolio Industry Exclusions	SPUS	0.49%	Growth
ShariaPortfolio Global Sukuk	SPSK	0.65%	Capital Preservation
ShariaPortfolio Global REIT	SPRE	0.69%	Sector (Real Estate)
Wealthsimple World Equity	WSHR	N/A	Growth
iShares USA Islamic	ISUS	0.50%	Growth
iShares World Islamic	ISWD	0.60%	Growth

If you'd like to invest in any of these ETFs, you can simply purchase via your online brokerage account.

Unconventional Wisdom

In this chapter I'd like to discuss a variety of other investment choices that are less common than stocks and funds. Some of these are permissible, some fall into gray areas, and some are prohibited. I'll specify as I go along, but the latter items are meant for awareness.

The ABCs of ESPPs

I already spent a lot of time talking about stocks in Chapter 3, but there is another related item I'd like to mention. If you work for a publicly traded company, and assuming the company is *Shariah*-compliant as an investment (you can look up the company using the Zoya app), see if it offers an Employee Stock Purchase Plan (ESPP).

An ESPP allows the employee to purchase shares of company stock at a discounted price in return for payroll deductions. I see ESPPs as a win-win, as the company gets to hold onto more cash in the interim and employees are incentivized to help the company perform well since they will be shareholders (that is, part owners) of the company.

Plan details will vary by company, but I'll provide an example to illustrate how an ESPP works. Let's say your company offers this and they have an offering period of six months. We can assume January to June and July to December to keep it simple. Employees can enroll before an offering period begins and determine what percentage of their pay they'd like deducted, or withheld, to be put towards the eventual stock purchase. The Internal Revenue Service (IRS) currently allows a max contribution of $25,000 per year towards an ESPP, so you'll have to keep that in mind when picking a percentage.

If you choose, say, a 10% contribution to the ESPP, gross pay would be reduced by 10% for each paycheck during the offering period. The company will hold onto this money and use it to conduct business and hopefully grow the company. At the end of the offering period, all that money that was deducted from your paychecks and "saved up" will be used to purchase company stock on your behalf.

But here's the beauty of it: Not only do you get the stocks at a discount (which can be up to 15%

off market price), the discount may be calculated on the lower of the stock prices at the beginning and end of the offering period.

If we assume the stock price was $100 on January 1st and $110 on June 30th, and sticking with the 15% discount, you'd get each stock for only $85. Even though the discount was only 15%, you essentially have a gain of 29.4% because the current market price is $110. After the offering period ends and you take possession of the stocks, you can sell them right away and enjoy the profits, or you can hold onto the stocks if you expect further growth in the future. If you do sell, you'll have to pay a capital gains tax on the profits. To estimate how much you might owe in capital gains taxes, use an online calculator like smartasset.com/investing/capital-gains-tax-calculator.

Sukuk Explained At Last

I've mentioned *sukuk* several times already in previous chapters but avoided any real explanation of it. If the suspense was making you anxious and you were on the edge of your seat wanting to know what *sukuk* are, you can relax now. The time has finally come.

Sukuk are the Islamic equivalent of bonds. The way a conventional bond works is that you buy a bond from a company or government in order to provide them a loan. They promise to pay back that loan in the form of principal + interest. Bonds involve *riba*.

Companies can sell *sukuk* for the same purpose, to raise capital, with the intention of paying back principal along with small distributions that are not fixed amounts like percentage-based interest. These distributions are a form of profit-sharing. *Sukuk* are asset-backed, not simply promise-backed. Said assets are used to grow the business and generate revenue. Risk is shared between the two parties, unlike a typical lender-lendee relationship.

The other similarity with bonds is that *sukuk* are considered a pretty stable and safe investment, a nice way to diversify one's portfolio. Returns aren't high, but that's not the main objective. The purpose is capital preservation. *Sukuk* can also be a good option for the risk-averse investor.

If you're interested in investing in *sukuk*, check out the capital preservation funds I discussed in the previous chapter.

Options for the Future

Futures and options are both considered derivatives. A futures contract is an agreement to buy or sell something on a future date, although the price is agreed on in the present time. The goal is to insure, or hedge, against the risk of drastic price fluctuations in the future. Commodities (i.e. raw materials like oil, corn, rice) are often invested in via futures contracts.

Let's say you enter into a futures contract to buy potatoes at $0.75/lb. If potatoes soar in popularity thanks to innovative new dishes introduced by YouTube and TikTok influencers, you can take advantage and sell at the current market price of, say, $1.25/lb. Then again, if demand is down and/or there's an overabundance of potatoes, perhaps the price will dip to $0.50/lb. In that case, the seller of the futures contract benefits. It's all a gamble.

There's also concern around whether or not the seller actually has possession of the commodity being referenced in the futures contract. The same issue comes up with dropshipping and shorting stocks. Because of these reasons, many scholars say futures contracts are impermissible.

It was reported by Abdullah ibn 'Amr (AS) that Prophet Muhammad (SAW) said: "It is not permissible to arrange a loan combined with a sale, or to stipulate two conditions in one transaction, or to make a profit on something that is not under your control, or to sell something that you do not possess." [Tirmidhi]

Stock options are similar to futures in that there's an agreement to buy shares of stock in the future if a particular market price is reached. Suppose there's a company called Potatoes for the People Inc. Shares are currently trading at $40. You enter into a stock options contract to purchase 100 shares if the price reaches $45. Thanks to your social media savviness, you believe the price will eventually hit $50/share. If and when the price hits $45, you can exercise the option and purchase, then wait until the market price hits $50 to sell at a profit. If the contract has not yet expired, you could even wait until the market price hits $50 while still being able to exercise the option and purchase at the lower, agreed price of $45.

Stock options are kind of like buying a lottery ticket. There's a fee to enter into such a contract. If the stock price never reaches the agreed price, the investor can simply let the contract expire and forego the cost of entering into that contract. That's because he/she purchased the right to buy those shares of stock, but not the obligation to. Since futures and options are highly speculative, I personally think they're better to avoid.

The Annuity Trap

I see annuities as an insurance product rather than an investment. Annuities are one way to prepare for retirement. I'll deep-dive on retirement plans in the following chapter, but let me give you a quick overview of annuities here.

Annuities are plans in which you make payments to an insurance company. After reaching a certain age, the insurance company will begin sending you monthly or annual payments for the remainder of your life.

Scholars seem to be in agreement that annuities are impermissible. They're effectively a gamble because no one knows how long they'll live. If you live only a few years after retirement, the insurance company benefits because they get to keep the remainder of the money. If you end up living a very long life, you might get more money out of the insurance company than you put in. Both parties are betting against one another.

The insurance company is doing plenty of calculations and structuring these in a way that will be profitable for them. The company might use your premiums to invest in things like interest-bearing bonds. There are also fees associated with having annuities. Annuities don't exist for altruistic reasons.

Getting Real About Real Estate

If you have the means, real estate provides a lucrative investment opportunity as well as diversification. There will always be a need for housing, and homes in good communities with low crime and high-performing schools will appreciate or at least hold their value.

After the Great Pandemic of 2020 and the increased ability to work from home, hordes of people moved out of expensive, cramped urban dwellings to suburban and even rural communities. Supply and demand kicked in and it became a seller's market. A housing shortage caused people to outbid one another on homes, leading the winners to pay more for a house than it was really worth.

If real estate sounds like something up your alley, you have a few options. You can purchase a commercial property and lease out storefronts to prospective business owners. Or you can purchase an apartment building, condominium, or house and rent it out to tenants. This will give you an ongoing revenue stream, but remember that as the owner/landlord you'll be responsible for repairs, property taxes, etc. Alternatively, you could purchase a fixer-upper home, renovate it, and then resell it with a mark-up.

There are a number of things to keep in mind, such as initial home inspection, homeowners insurance, the repairs or renovations needed (if any), the process of selling the home or finding tenants, and upkeep of the investment property. As you probably learned in school, location, location, and location are three of the most important things. Aside from crime rates and quality of schools, also consider proximity to highways and train stations. If you're planning on renting out, you need to have a contract template for leases, and think about how you would handle bad tenants if issues arise.

Also remember that revenue earned from rental properties is taxable income. Not to scare you, but another thing to be aware of is liability. If a tenant sues you and you're simply a sole proprietor, he/she could come after your personal wealth and assets, which is why savvy real estate investors set up limited liability companies (LLCs) through which they conduct business, or purchase liability insurance.

Just as a word of warning, I would also like to remind people about the housing bubble and subsequent crash we saw in the US in 2008.

People were buying homes beyond their means, and banks were approving them for large loans with exorbitant interest rates. These were known as subprime mortgages. Eventually it all came crashing down with people defaulting on loans, leading to foreclosures. Sadly, there were people counting on this downfall. These subprime mortgages were packaged up and sold as mortgage-backed securities to unassuming investors, while hedge funds bet against these securities.

The point is that you should be aware of general economic conditions and housing market conditions before venturing into this space. Do your research and be mindful of the risks. I also recommend performing *istikhara* prayer before making big decisions.

As for buying the property, you can use cash or take out a loan from a *Shariah*-compliant mortgage company such as Guidance Residential (guidanceresidential.com) or UIF (myuif.com) in the US. Canada and the UK also have similar companies such as Manzil (manzil.ca) and Al Rayan (alrayanbank.co.uk), respectively.

If all of this sounds like too much of a headache or more responsibility than you'd care to take on, yet you're still hungry for a slice of the pie, there's still hope in the form of Real Estate Investment Trusts (REITs).

REITs are firms that own commercial and/or residential properties, and use those properties to generate revenue via long-term leases, short-term leases, and sometimes interest income in the case of mortgage REITs. The properties are not just homes, offices, and stores, but can also include storage facilities and telecommunication tower sites.

An REIT fund is basically a fund that contains REIT firms. Just like any mutual fund or ETF, there's some level of diversification built in and risk is spread across the various firms the fund invests in. Investors' money is pooled to invest in REIT firms. Such funds can provide long-term growth as well as dividend income.

Unfortunately there haven't been many *Shariah*-compliant REITs in the US, but hopefully this market will grow. Azzad has had an REIT portfolio since 2004. However, they require interested investors to enroll in their Azzad Ethical Wrap Program in order to access the REIT portfolio. This is a full-fledged investment management program with a $500,000 minimum investment.

A more accessible option is ShariaPortfolio's SP Funds S&P Global REIT Sharia ETF, which went live at the end of 2020. Since it's an exchange-traded fund, any investor can purchase it via an online brokerage service. It trades under the ticker symbol SPRE.

Another option in the US is Soho Properties, which has specialized in New York City properties since 2003. They advise interested investors on new investment opportunities. These are typically big-ticket investments, and a minimum preferred investment can be $100,000. Details will vary by project. Projects can include developing new properties for commercial and/or residential use, acquiring existing properties, or buying out a mezzanine loan. In speaking with the founder and one of his associates, I learned that most of their clients are doctors. If this would be of interest to you, check out their website sohoproperties.com to learn more and get in touch with them.

Adventures in Venture Capital

An exciting option for investing is startups. Startups are new, hopefully up-and-coming companies offering innovative products or services brought forth by entrepreneurs. As you can imagine, such a venture requires lots of capital for development, marketing, etc. to really gain traction. These entrepreneurs can seek funding from venture capitalists, angel investors, or crowdfunding platforms like Kickstarter.

The major caveat with startup investing is that you could lose it all. There's no guarantee the startup will succeed. These companies aren't established, nor are they publicly traded. You'll have limited info on their financials, and the founder(s) may have limited experience. Aside from the obvious screening of their product or service for *Shariah*-compliance, you'll have to do your part in researching and making a sound judgement as to whether there are any issues with the company. On a positive note, the folks asking for funding are usually pretty accessible and open to questions.

There are many platforms you can scour for startup investing opportunities. Two sites worth exploring are StartEngine (startengine.com) and Republic (republic.co). It's free to sign up for either site and you have to provide identification, but even without signing up you can browse opportunities. If there's a startup you'd like to invest in, you can use a credit card on StartEngine or link your bank account on Republic.

A newcomer in the crowdfunding space, one designed specifically for *halal* investment opportunities, is Fursa Capital, having launched in early 2021. After signing up and providing identification, you can browse opportunities and invest after funding your account. Fursa's website is fursacapital.com.

If you're outside of the US, there's a company called Ethis you can look into. When I checked with them at the end of 2020, they advised that they "do not accept investors from the USA simply because of the complexity and barriers imposed by the US government on foreign investment companies." It is open to investors from many other countries, though.

In any case, Ethis offers *Shariah*-compliant crowdfunding for various projects, some real estate-related, some not. If you go to ethis.co/id, you can view the available campaigns in Indonesia. After signing up on their site, you have to complete your profile and provide identification.

Another *Shariah*-compliant, international option is Kapital Boost. Like Ethis, it focuses on opportunities in Asian countries. Not all offerings are businesses. This crowdfunding platform can also be used for fundraising campaigns. Kapital's website is kapitalboost.com.

For the Brits, there's Intro Crowd (introcrowd.com) and Seedrs (seedrs.com). The latter is similar to StartEngine and you can browse opportunities without having to register. Intro Crowd is a little different. It's an investing platform for land, or what they refer to as strategic land. That land can then be used for development projects like housing. Although Intro Crowd is not a Muslim company, it has a Shariah Compliance Consultant on board.

Oh, and one other exciting thing I should mention is that if you're looking to start your own company, you can consider a platform like Fursa, StartEngine, or Seedrs to help you raise funds instead of taking out a loan. Another company that allows you to request funding, whether it's to start a business or fulfill some other personal need, is BFF Income Share Funding. Their website is fundmebff.com.

My Precious

A fun way to expand your investment portfolio is by purchasing precious metals like gold, silver, copper, platinum, or palladium. Precious metals can be purchased in the form of coins, bars, or jewelry. Rather than something intangible like stocks, you have something physical and shiny that you can hold in your hands. And if the need arises, you can sell or trade metals relatively easily.

Gold has been an object of beauty and value for millennia. It's something that has historically held its value very well. Did you know that US currency used to be backed by gold? Unfortunately, the Great Depression helped kibosh that because people traded in paper currency and began hoarding gold. In turn, the US government ordered Americans to turn in their gold (other than small amounts) in 1933 in exchange for paper currency. This marked the beginning of the end for the gold standard. US currency is now considered fiat currency, meaning it's not backed by any commodity.

If you'd like to purchase metals online rather than a local brick-and-mortar shop, two legitimate sellers are Apmex (apmex.com) and JM Bullion (jmbullion.com). As a reminder, *Zakat* (alms) is due on gold and silver, while scholars generally agree that other metals including platinum and palladium are exempt.

Needless to say, there is some risk in storing precious metals in your home, as the home could be burglarized or fall prey to a natural disaster that results in a loss. Of course, you could buy insurance, but the general consensus on conventional insurance (as opposed to *takaful*) is that it's impermissible unless it's legally required in your country/state (such as health or automobile insurance) or required by some other entity (such as homeowners insurance required by a homeowner association).

If you don't want the risk of storing precious metals at home, you can look into commodity-based mutual funds or ETFs that focus on metals (either on holding physical metals or on mining for such metals). For example, SPDR Gold Shares (GLD) and SPDR Gold MiniShares (GLDM) are two ETFs that are considered *Shariah*-compliant at time of writing.

The Effects of FX

Investing in foreign currency, or Forex as it's commonly referred to, is yet another way to diversify. It's not without risk, though. As you know, the world is filled with a variety of currencies since each country came up with a common form of exchange at some point in its history. Naturally, we need something widely accepted as holding value that we can earn and subsequently trade for products and services.

We live in a global economy, and money is being exchanged between countries all day, every day. Between international trade, geopolitical factors, economic stability, supply and demand, and other factors, the value of one currency against another is in constant flux. For instance, $10 US currency might get you £7 British pounds today, but £8 British pounds tomorrow. Why the sudden change? It could be that the US dollar strengthened in value and/or the British pound weakened in value. Either way, these ups and downs are normal.

This is where investing in Forex comes in, as there's an opportunity to capitalize on these fluctuations. In short, the investor aims to buy a currency while it's weak, then sell it after it strengthens in value. To be clear, the investor isn't literally buying another currency and doesn't take possession of it, but I'm trying to keep this simple.

Forex trading involves currency pairs, like GBP/USD. I'll provide a more detailed example to better illustrate the process. Suppose you open a 50:1 account with a Forex broker. You plop down $1,000, but the brokerage allows you to invest $50,000. Say you invest the whole shebang in GBP/USD and the current exchange rate is 1.40. This gives you £35,714.29 in British currency ($50,000 / 1.40). The exchange rate then rises to 1.50. You can now sell the British currency for $53,571.43 in US currency (£35,714.29 x 1.5). You have to pay back the $49,000 loan to the broker. Still, it appears you made a whopping $3,571.43 in profit. Well, almost. First you have to pay the broker a commission and any other fees they may have charged. It also shouldn't come as a surprise that capital gains taxes are due on profits.

Is Forex trading permissible? My opinion is that Forex is speculative and similar to gambling, as the investor is betting on one currency against another. Further, Forex is usually done via leverage, or margin, as illustrated in the prior example. This is because Forex trading is only worthwhile with large sums of money due to the minute fluctuations in exchange rates. To obtain this large sum of money, Forex investors typically take out a loan from a broker for the purpose of trading foreign currency. The investor has to hope they'll profit enough to pay back this loan and keep the change.

The Cryptic World of Crypto

Cryptocurrency is basically digital or virtual currency. Unlike most currencies, it's not backed or regulated by any central authority. It's decentralized. No banks or governments are involved. Transactions involving cryptocurrency are recorded in digital ledgers called blockchains. This ensures security and prevents counterfeiting, as power is given to the people to manage the currency. Online transactions using cryptocurrency can be made anonymously, although transactions are traceable.

Is it permissible? Islamically speaking, everything is *halal* unless and until it's proven to be *haram*, so I can only offer my opinion here.

I'm perfectly fine with moving from paper currency to digital currency, but I have a couple of concerns with cryptocurrency *as an investment*. I don't like the idea of investing in a currency, as the purpose of currency should be to exchange it for something else of value. It's not really a commodity like gold or silver, though some would argue it's both a currency and a commodity. There's some ambiguity around its nature, not to mention its origin. But to be fair, gold and silver were used as currency in the past and are now considered commodities, so it's acceptable for something to evolve.

All currencies fluctuate in value due to inflation and other factors, but that's part of the ebb and flow of the global economy. Bitcoin is arguably the most popular, and the original, cryptocurrency. It had a market value of roughly $8,000 at the start of 2020, and jumped to roughly $38,000 at the beginning of 2021. Most currencies don't fluctuate at this velocity unless there's major social or political upheaval. A single Tweet can greatly impact the price of Bitcoin. And this is for one single "coin", though thankfully it's possible to buy a portion of a Bitcoin (similar to fractional shares of stocks).

Some scholars have claimed that crypto is *haram*, while others say it's *halal*. To be clear, I'm not stating it's *haram*, but I would summarize my concerns as follows:

Investing in a currency is speculative, which is akin to gambling. It was presented as a currency and did previously get used as a currency on

Silk Road and such, but now people are investing in it to make a quick buck. It's being treated more like a commodity, but doesn't have the same utility as a physical commodity. The underlying technology, blockchain, does have benefits, but many current investors don't really care about that nor necessarily understand it. The technology can exist without an overlaying currency. It would be nice to have a single, universal digital currency, but with so many cryptocurrencies popping up, it brings to mind old "pump and dump" schemes.

Based on the available scholarly opinions, you're welcome to make your own decision on whether or not to invest in crypto. Having said that, the Fiqh Council of North America ruled that Bitcoin is permissible because the evidence to claim otherwise is not strong enough. Further, Islamic Finance Guru has a running list of cryptocurrencies along with their *halal* status. View their list at islamicfinanceguru.com/crypto.

There are now many different cryptocurrencies available. Bitcoin, Ethereum, and Litecoin are a few of the most popular, but there's also

Polkadot, Chainlink, and Neo. I still find it humorous that Dogecoin was created as a joke, but now it's considered a legitimate crypto.

You might be wondering how money is even made on cryptocurrency, as it's quite different than investing in an equity stock. One way an investor can make money is simply by buying and holding (affectionately called "HODLing") until the value increases, then selling. Value can increase due to supply and demand (as there are limits on the number of "coins" that will be available) or hype surrounding a particular crypto.

Another method is staking. The easiest way to explain staking is that you "lock up" your cryptocurrency for a set period of time. You are then rewarded for your participation with additional "coins". What's the purpose of staking? It helps the crypto ecosystem by forging a block in the digital ledger. This helps validate transactions using a consensus method called proof-of-stake. Remember, it's the people who are collectively managing a cryptocurrency, not some central bank. Before entering into a staking contract, I would urge you to review the terms of the agreement to ensure interest is not involved as a reward.

A third way to make money is by lending crypto, which may be referred to as centralized staking. However, this is essentially the digital version of a savings account with a standard bank, where you lend money and earn interest in return. Naturally, this should be avoided due to *riba*.

As for how to invest in or buy crypto, you can either invest in the currency directly or via crypto futures. The latter should be avoided in my opinion for the reasons I discussed earlier in this chapter on futures contracts.

An easy way to purchase crypto is via a PayPal account. If you have a PayPal account, simply log in and click on Crypto to select from a few of the popular (but limited) choices. Certain online brokerages such as Robinhood also allow you to buy and sell crypto in addition to stocks and ETFs.

Power users will want to opt for a crypto exchange. Such platforms have a wide array of cryptocurrencies to choose from. A popular platform in the US is Coinbase (coinbase.com). The company actually went public in April 2021, so investors can not only invest in cryptocurrencies, but in an actual exchange or marketplace if they want to. Signing up with a platform such as Coinbase is similar to signing up with any online brokerage; provide your info and identification, then link your bank account so you can buy and sell. There are transaction fees for buying and selling, by the way.

After purchasing cryptocurrency, you have to store it in a digital wallet. This can either be online (such as with a platform like Coinbase), offline on your computer, on a mobile device, or on a small physical device that you can carry around with you.

There's a lot more to crypto, and it's an area that's continuing to grow and mature, but hopefully this gives you a glimpse into the topic.

The Bizarre World of NFTs

Would you ever pay half a million dollars for an animated, digital image of a cat? Would you believe someone actually did pay over $500,000 for an animated GIF of Nyan Cat? Did you know that Twitter founder Jack Dorsey sold his very first tweet for $2.9 million? Welcome to the bizarre world of non-fungible tokens (NFTs).

NFTs are digital assets like images or audio files that utilize blockchain technology to guarantee authenticity and uniqueness. This is a way to ensure that the owner has the purest, most original form of a digital asset, whereas all those other images floating around the internet of the same exact thing are merely copies. Big deal, right?

Are they permissible? As with crypto, it's most likely *halal* unless proven otherwise. I personally believe NFTs are a gray area and that we will see varying scholarly opinions. The thing is, art is not inherently impermissible. Just as an oil painting of Arabic calligraphy is perfectly fine, a digital version would be just as fine. If a digital image contains things contrary to Islamic values and is being auctioned off as an NFT, then it could be argued that this particular NFT is *haram*.

Again, I'm no scholar, so take the following with a grain of salt. Based on some of the high-dollar NFT sales by celebrities and YouTubers, I see NFTs as wasteful spending that risks venturing into *israf* (extravagance) while providing no real value, purpose, or utility other than personal satisfaction. There are other intangible things that do hold value like trademarks and intellectual property, but value is earned and built up over time, or IP is transformed into something useful and practical. However, it would also be fair for someone to argue that buying an NFT is no different than buying a fine piece of art, and that if someone has the means to do so, there's no harm in it.

I also **worry** that value is being artificially inflated through hype. The founders and people with popularity can ride the wave and cash in on the hype, but eventually that wave will die down, leaving buyers with bragging rights but not much else. Who knows, maybe they'll be able to collect royalties by having ownership of a certain character, graphic, or soundbite. At some point a new fad will come along and perhaps NFTs will no longer hold such high value.

Then again, this could be the future of art and not much different than having possession of a genuine Van Gogh painting rather than a reproduction or print. Maybe NFTs are the solution for preserving digital art. Just as an art collector would pay a handsome sum for a one-of-a-kind painting, a digital art collector can do the same with an NFT. We'll have to wait and see how it plays out in the long-term.

If you're interested in investing in NFTs, it's not like stocks or funds. You can't log into a brokerage app and simply buy one. These are unique digital assets sold on niche platforms like SuperRare (superrare.co), Nifty Gateway (niftygateway.com), Mintable (mintable.app), Rarible (rarible.com), and Crypto (crypto.com/nft). You'll need to own some cryptocurrency like Ethereum and connect your digital wallet to the platform. You can then buy an NFT and hope that it will increase in value so you can sell it later for a profit. Whether or not a particular NFT will increase in value, well, it's a gamble.

Desire to Retire

For those of us working corporate jobs, wouldn't it be nice some day to get out of the rat race and do whatever we want with our time? Soon enough *insha'Allah*, but until then we should at least begin planning for retirement, even if it seems far away.

Some might say that there's no guarantee we will even live that long, so why bother? Others may depend on their kids to take care of them in old age. And some might depend on government programs or pensions to cover their needs.

Well, nothing is guaranteed. But if we do end up living long lives, shouldn't we put some effort into being independent and self-sufficient? Just like we can't predict how long we'll live, we also can't predict how our children will treat us decades from now, nor if government social security programs will have funding left.

Government-Sponsored Programs

In the US, the government collects Social Security taxes from workers. During tax season, people will receive a W-2 form from their employer that lists the various deductions taken from their gross pay, including Social Security tax.

The government then distributes this money on a monthly basis to eligible folks, such as retirees and disabled people. People can apply for Social Security benefits between age 62 and 70. The longer a person waits, the higher the monthly payout is. Other countries have similar programs.

The concept is nice. Those of us who are young, healthy, and employed put money into a system that benefits those who have already done their time. Then future generations will do the same for us when we're old...maybe.

I have a couple of concerns with Social Security. For one, it wasn't designed to entirely replace one's living expenses. According to the American Association of Retired Persons (AARP), the estimated average payout in 2021 was $1,543 per month. Depending on where you live in the US, that amount may or may not get you very far.

The other thing is that life expectancy has risen from about 68 years in 1950 to roughly 79 years in 2021. That's great. But it also means that because people are living longer, they're continuing to receive Social Security benefits and thereby depleting funds. It certainly doesn't mean the program will be totally bankrupt by the time you retire, but my suggestion is to not be dependent on any such benefits.

Employer-Sponsored Programs

In the old days, pensions were much more common. If you work for a certain type of organization like a public school or government agency, you might still have access to a pension plan. Labor unions may also still use pension plans.

Pensions are plans where the employer contributes money to a fund. Employees may or may not be contributing to the fund. The employer manages the program and takes on all risk and responsibility involved, but may hire a professional investment firm to manage the portfolio. As workers begin to retire, the company will distribute monthly payouts to them.

Unless the company happens to be an investment firm, managing a pension plan is not the company's core competency and therefore easier and less risky to outsource. There is where 401(k)s come into play. Employers can offer a 401(k), but they don't have to worry about managing it or funding it necessarily. There are many 401(k) providers a company can choose from, such as Fidelity, T. Rowe Price, Vanguard, Edward Jones, Voya Financial, etc.

With a 401(k), the employee has the option to utilize it or not. The employee can decide what percentage of his pre-tax income he would like to contribute to his 401(k), which will be deducted from his paycheck. The employee will even have a few choices as to where the money is invested.

The 401(k) equivalent for non-profit or tax-exempt organizations is a 403(b), while local governments have the 457(b). These are all essentially the same thing. Employers can tout these plans as a benefit, and employees get an easy way to begin investing towards retirement. It's a win-win.

What's the Big Deal?

The major advantage of something like a 401(k) is that contributions are tax-deferred. This means that the money you put into a 401(k) from your paycheck will not be taxed in the present time. Your taxable income in the present time is effectively reduced. Only after you retire and begin withdrawing money will it be taxed as income.

Another nice perk with 401(k)s is that your employer might match your contributions up to a certain percent. Suppose your bi-weekly gross pay is $2,000 and you choose to contribute 5% towards your 401(k). That means $100 of every paycheck goes towards your 401(k). If the company offers 100% matching, you get an extra $100 added to your 401(k) courtesy of your employer. If they only offer 50% matching, you still get an extra $50 per pay period added to your 401(k).

The downside is that you can't touch the money until you retire, unless you jump through some hoops and are willing to incur tax penalties and/or early withdrawal penalties. Further, the US government limits how much you can contribute to a 401(k).

There are a couple of other things to be aware of. Some people don't like 401(k)s because of the management fees. Providers aren't going to manage these for free. It's similar to mutual funds where they deduct a small percentage from your total assets. Larger companies tend to incur smaller fees from providers, while smaller companies incur higher fees. On average, fees can range from .5% to 2%.

Additionally, you'll have limited choices for where your money is invested. Let's say the 401(k) provider is Vanguard. They may only offer employees a handful of funds to choose from. Some might be equity funds, and some may contain bonds (which, once again, are interest-bearing).

Can I Opt Out?

If you'd like to opt out of a 401(k) or similar retirement savings program, or if your employer doesn't even offer such a program, you can go with an Individual Retirement Account (IRA) instead.

Why would someone want to opt out of a company-sponsored program, especially if the company is providing a matching contribution? One reason is that you will have limited investment choices with a 401(k), meaning it's possible your 401(k) is not *Shariah*-compliant. You'll have much more control over where your money is invested with an IRA. If you're willing to give up company matching for the sake of being *Shariah*-compliant with your retirement savings, that's excellent. Another reason is that you'll likely have lower account management fees with an IRA.

Before opting out of a 401(k), it's worth asking your Human Resources department or Benefits Coordinator if there's an option for a self-directed or self-brokered account. If so, this would give you flexibility to invest your money where you like, while still enjoying a company contribution towards that account.

What Exactly is an IRA?

An Individual Retirement Account is a self-managed retirement account. Neither your employer nor a third-party benefits administrator will manage it for you. You're responsible for opening the account, putting money into it, and choosing where exactly the money is invested. It's a good option if you're self-employed or if your employer doesn't have a retirement program, as stated earlier.

An IRA can be opened through any online brokerage or investment firm, including those that offer mutual funds. An IRA is similar to a 401(k) in that you can't withdraw money until a certain age, and it can be tax-deferred.

What Types of IRAs are Available?

There are a few flavors of IRA, including one designed for minors. The two main types of IRA, though, are Traditional and Roth. The primary difference between the two is related to taxes, namely *when* taxes are incurred.

Whatever money you contribute to a Traditional IRA, you can deduct when you file your annual taxes. Those contributions reduce your taxable income. After you retire and begin withdrawing money, it'll be considered income and therefore taxable. Until then, taxes are deferred on those contributions.

With a Roth IRA, you cannot deduct contributions from your taxes. Whatever money you put into a Roth IRA from your income, it's still considered part of your current year's income and you'll have to pay taxes on it. The upside? After you retire and withdraw money, it'll be tax-free income.

The question is: Do you want to take the tax hit now or later? Either way, the tax man cometh, and there's no definitive answer on which type of IRA is better.

How Much Money Can I Put into a Retirement Account?

The maximum annual contribution can change by the year, but as of 2021 the max contribution for a 401(k) is $19,500. If you're over age 50, though, you can contribute an additional $6,500, known as a "catch-up" contribution.

When it comes time to figure out what percentage of your paycheck you should put into your 401(k), one way to go about it is to divide your max contribution by your salary. Let's suppose you're age 40 and have a salary of $75,000. $19,500 divided by $75,000 is 26%. You definitely don't have to max it out, but 26% would be the highest deduction you could do without risking over-contribution.

With either a Traditional or Roth IRA, you can contribute $6,000 annually if you're under age 50. If you're 50 or older, the max annual contribution is $7,000. If you happen to have both a Traditional and Roth IRA, bear in mind that these figures represent the total contribution across all of your IRAs.

There is another stipulation to be cognizant of. The Roth IRA becomes less appealing the higher your income gets. If you're single and making less than $125,000 per year in gross income (based on 2021 figures), Roth is fine. If you're married (filing joint returns) and making less than $198,000 combined in gross income, Roth is still fine. Once you exceed those figures, either your max IRA contributions become limited or you're not eligible at all for a Roth. Traditional would be the way to go in that case.

The higher your income gets, the more recommended it is to seek professional advice from a financial advisor or tax consultant. They can help you maximize retirement savings without running afoul of IRS rules like having to pay a penalty for excess contributions.

When Can I Withdraw Money?

When you retire and want to finally dip into those hard-earned savings, you can begin taking distributions. You can decide the rate of withdrawal, although 4% is often touted as the golden number.

Suppose you have $1 million in your 401(k) or IRA at retirement. A 4% distribution would be $40,000, hopefully enough to cover your living expenses for a year. The $960,000 that remains in your 401(k) will continue to grow since it will remain invested in whichever funds you had chosen.

The minimum age you can begin to take distributions is 59½. If you withdraw money prior to this age, you'll incur a 10% penalty. Remember, taxes will be due on distributions taken from a 401(k) or Traditional IRA, but not for a Roth IRA.

Although the minimum age is 59½, you could choose to leave your retirement account alone and let it continue to grow if you're still working. However, if you have a 401(k) or Traditional IRA, you *have* to begin taking distributions by age 72 because the government wants its tax income. This rule does not apply to Roth IRAs; taxes are already paid, so the government doesn't really care if you withdraw money or leave it sitting there.

Rollovers

Suppose you have a 401(k) that you'd like to convert to an IRA. Again, this could be for the sake of *Shariah*-compliance so you can choose where the money is invested, or you simply have an old 401(k) from a previous employer that you want to consolidate with an existing IRA. You could also transition a 401(k) from a previous employer to a new employer's plan, or transfer from one IRA to another IRA if you want to consolidate or switch providers.

In any case, the process known as rollover isn't terribly complicated. It essentially involves opening an IRA with a new provider, providing permission to your 401(k) administrator to liquidate funds, and then transferring those funds into your new IRA. Once the funds are there, you can decide exactly where to invest those funds.

The process can involve filling out one or more forms, but I was able to roll over a 401(k) over the phone. I'll share my experience here.

I decided to go with Wahed, so I scheduled a call with a representative. He set up a three-way call between us and my 401(k) administrator. I confirmed my information and gave consent to liquidate the account (i.e. full payout), after which the 401(k) company sent me a check that was made payable to a clearing house. It took about a week to receive the check.

In the meantime, I opened an IRA via Wahed's website and took their quiz to determine my risk profile, which determines how much money goes into Wahed's ETF vs. *sukuk*, gold, and cash. After receiving the check, I wrote my Wahed account number on it and mailed it to the clearing house. The clearing house deposited the check, after which the funds became available in my Wahed account.

How Much is Enough?

Only Allah (SWT) knows our remaining time in this life. Because we have no idea how many years we have left, it becomes difficult to plan financially for our retirement years. Since we can't easily access funds in a retirement account until we reach a certain age, it feels like the money is being held hostage. We may end up enjoying only some of the retirement money we spent decades saving, or perhaps none at all.

One could take the *carpe diem* approach and live for today, putting her money in liquid assets only. Or one could put all of her savings into retirement accounts with the hopes of living large some day while living frugally now.

My advice is to take a balanced approach. Put some money into liquid investments with the intention of long-term savings, but with the option to withdraw early if needed without penalty. And put some into retirement accounts to enjoy tax deferment. I'm not necessarily saying to do a 50-50 split, as everyone's situation is different. Think about savings for short-term (i.e. a new car or *Hajj*), mid-term (i.e. a house), and long-term (i.e. retirement). If your short-term needs happen to outweigh long-term needs, then for now it's probably best to focus on liquid investments that you can easily withdraw/cash out if needed.

Plan to save more than you think you'll need for retirement, but don't go overboard with it. If you die shortly after retirement, the money you saved up can go to family or even to a charitable organization (which is why it's important to list beneficiaries and have a will). But if you happen to live for many years post-retirement, *insha'Allah* you'll have enough money to live comfortably.

Another thing to keep in mind is that today's dollars do not equal tomorrow's dollars. Remember that thing called inflation I talked about earlier in this book? Just something to keep in mind.

Rather than give a specific dollar amount, as cost of living varies throughout the world and even in different parts of one country, I'd recommend that you play around with online retirement calculators and/or spreadsheets to estimate how much you need. Once you have a figure, you can work backwards in planning how to achieve it, as well as break down how much you want to put into locked retirement accounts vs. liquid investments.

There are many online calculators available, and they each incorporate different factors and calculations. Thus, you'll end up with a hodgepodge of "how much you will need" figures. Still, these calculators are fun to play around with and give you some idea of your "number". The ones I recommend are:

- SmartAsset: This one factors in your location
    - smartasset.com/retirement/retirement-calculator
- NerdWallet: Basic, but click on Optional to add more details
    - nerdwallet.com/investing/retirement-calculator
- AARP: This one takes your spouse into consideration
    - aarp.org/work/retirement-planning/retirement_calculator.html

Do your part to prepare for the future – tie your camel – and leave the rest in Allah's (SWT) hands. Don't fret too much.

Famous Last Words

To wrap up, I'd like to leave you with some parting advice as you pursue your *halal* wealth journey.

Don't think of money as the root of all evil. Greed is bad, but money is simply a tool or resource. What you do with it, whether good or bad, is up to you. As the old saying goes, let money remain in your hands, not in your heart. Don't let money become your idol.

Remember that your wealth could act as a witness against you on the Day of Judgement, and that no amount of wealth will guarantee you a spot in *Jannah* (Heaven).

"Now, whenever a human being is tested by their Lord through His generosity and blessings, they boast, 'My Lord has deservedly honoured me!' But when He tests them by limiting their provision, they protest, 'My Lord has undeservedly humiliated me!' Absolutely not! In fact, you are not even gracious to the orphan, nor do you urge one another to feed the poor. And you devour others' inheritance greedily, and love wealth fervently." [89:15-20]

Don't think of money as finite. Money is just numbers. It's all digital nowadays, anyway. If you think there's only so much of a resource, you may try to tear others down to build yourself up. There's enough in this world for everyone. Food wastage is a simple example of this.

Think about why you want to invest. There are many worthy causes, whether it's providing for your family or taking them on *Hajj*. If you're only investing in something because there's currently a lot of fervor around it, you're investing for the wrong reason. It might be *Shariah*-compliant, but it's not necessarily values-based investing. It's based on a short-term desire to make a quick buck rather than build long-term value. Due diligence falls to the wayside in order to jump on the bandwagon before it passes by.

Avoid limiting beliefs. If you think you'll never earn a six-figure income, then you probably won't. On the other hand, if your goal is simply to avoid poverty and have enough to eat, then that may be all you achieve. Once again, our sustenance is already written for us, but I still say you should dream big. Be content with what you have while you work for what you want.

Don't let yourself get envious of others, and don't resent those who are wealthy. You can't really expect yourself to become wealthy if you have bitter feelings towards those who already are. Be happy for those who have already accomplished their goals, or at least don't allow yourself to harbor ill feelings for no logical reason.

Be cautious and avoid extravagance. Find a balance between enjoying nice things without going overboard, while also giving back. Extravagance can lead to arrogance, and arrogance is bad for your spiritual health.

It was reported by Abdullah ibn Mas'ud (AS) that Prophet Muhammad (SAW) said: "No one who has the weight of a seed of arrogance in his heart will enter Paradise." A man said, "But a man likes to have nice clothes and nice shoes." The Prophet said, "Verily, Allah is beautiful and He loves beauty. Arrogance is to disregard the truth and to look down upon people." [Muslim]

Be genuinely grateful for everything you have, and you will get more. It's easy to take things for granted, so you may need to remind yourself how much you truly have, whether it's your health, a home in a safe neighborhood, a reliable vehicle, etc.

"And remember when your Lord proclaimed, 'If you are grateful, I will certainly give you more…'" [14:7]

Be aware that *Zakat* is due not just on your cash-in-hand and gold/silver jewelry, but also on your investments. The rate of *Zakat* is 2.5%. Check out one of the following online calculators for help:

- Zakat Foundation: This one calculates in USD and is simple to use
    - zakat.org/resource-center/zakat-calculator
- National Zakat Foundation: This one calculates in CAD and considers Canada-specific retirement and educational savings plans
    - nzfcanada.com/calculate-zakat

- Islamic Finance Guru: This one calculates in GBP and factors in things like startups and crypto
    - zakat.islamicfinanceguru.com/calculator

Give *sadaqa* (charity). There are many organizations out there doing good work. Pick a cause that you care about and look up relevant organizations. Then check sites like Charity Navigator (charitynavigator.org) to see how they rate and how they're spending the funds they receive from donors (i.e. program expenses vs. administrative expenses). You can also find worthy causes on LaunchGood (launchgood.com).

While *Zakat* is an obligation, *sadaqa* is something you do from the goodness of your heart. *Sadaqa* is another opportunity to purify your wealth, and although it sounds counter-intuitive, it will not decrease your wealth. Quite the opposite, actually.

"The example of those who spend their wealth in the cause of God is that of a grain that sprouts into seven ears, each bearing one hundred grains. And God multiplies the reward even more to whoever He wills. For God is All-Bountiful, All-Knowing." [2:261]

Lastly, remember that it's not how *much* money you make; it's *how* you make it. A dollar earned through *halal* means will have greater *barakah* and will stretch further than a dollar earned through *haram* means.

I hope you found the information in this book useful. Anything good and beneficial is thanks to Allah (SWT), and any mistakes are mine. Let's make *niyyah* (intention) to invest and build wealth the *halal* way, and use our wealth to make the world a better place. I pray that you have the best of health, wealth, and happiness in this world and the Hereafter. *Ameen*.

Glossary

401(k): Retirement plan managed by a company for its employees; company may or may not match employee contributions

403(b): Retirement plan that's similar to a 401(k), but is specifically designed for organizations like public schools, places of worship, and certain non-profits

457(b): Retirement plan that's similar to a 401(k), but typically used by governmental organizations

Akhirah: The Hereafter, life to come

Allah: Arabic for God

Amortization: Loss of value on intangible assets, such as copyrights or other intellectual property; also used in reference to loans to describe the reduction in the principal amount of the loan as payments are made

AS: Acronym for *Alayhi Salaam*, meaning peace be upon him

Assets: Items that a person or business owns, such as machinery or equipment

Balance Sheet: A financial statement listing a company's assets, liabilities, and owner's equity;

the basic accounting equation is assets = liabilities + owner's equity

Bear Market: When market is "bearish", stock prices are falling and investors may sell off shares of stock

Bismillah: In the name of God

Blue-Chip Stocks: Stocks for large, established companies that have been around for a long time and are considered financially sound

Bonds: Essentially a loan to a company or government; bond certificates are typically sold in $1,000 increments; lendee makes interest payments regularly, and eventually pays back the principal amount once the term of the bond expires

Broker: One who buys/sells investments on the investor's behalf; charges a commission fee or management fee

Bull Market: When market is "bullish", stock prices are rising and investors are more confident about buying

Capital: Funds, or money, used for the purpose of starting or growing a business

Capital Gains Tax: Taxes due on profits realized by selling an investment

Certificate of Deposit (CD): Bank product in which you deposit money and it accrues interest over the term, but the depositor can't access the funds until the CD matures (i.e. the term ends)

Corporation: Type of business structure that is considered its own entity, separate from the owner(s); may be privately owned or publicly traded

Coupon Rate: The interest rate that is paid annually by a bond

Crypto: Cryptocurrency; digital money with no physical form, secured via encryption; rather than use a bank as a clearing house, uses a decentralized ledger called blockchain

Day Trading: Buying and selling shares of stock within the same day; considered speculative

Deen: Religion, faith

Depreciation: Loss of value on physical assets, such as machinery or equipment

Derivative: A contract that derives its value from underlying assets; futures contracts and options are examples of derivatives

Dividends: Periodic payout by some corporations from a portion of earnings as a way to reward shareholders; stocks may or may not pay dividends

Dow Jones Industrial Average (DJIA): Average of 30 different stocks that generally reflects the behavior of the entire stock market

Dua: Prayer, supplication, asking God for something

Dunya: This world, the present life

Equity: Ownership in an investment or other asset

Exchange Traded Funds (ETFs): Similar to mutual funds, but traded throughout the day on the stock market in the same manner as individual stocks; price may fluctuate throughout the day

Fatwa: Legal ruling on a certain matter per Islamic law

Foreclosure: When someone is unable to pay the mortgage on their home, the lender (typically a bank) can take over ownership of the home and then resell it; this causes a very negative impact to one's credit score

Forex: Short for foreign exchange

Futures: A futures contract is an agreement to buy or sell assets at a fixed price that is determined today, but delivery of and payment for the assets occurs in the future

Hajj: Pilgrimage to Mecca, one of the pillars of Islam

Halal: Permissible, acceptable

Haram: Forbidden, not allowed

Hedge Funds: Pooled money by a group of investors who use high-risk investing strategies to generate high returns

Ijara: The owner of an item (such as a house) "leases" to the customer, and the customer pays "rent" until the item is paid off

Income Statement: A financial statement detailing a company's revenues and expenses; revenues - expenses = net income (or net loss)

Individual Retirement Account (IRA): Retirement account set up by an individual person; variations include Traditional, Roth, SEP, and Simple

Insha'Allah: God willing

Investment Bank: Does not take deposits like a normal bank; provides financial services, such as selling securities and providing consulting on mergers and acquisitions

Istikhara: Special prayer one may perform to ask Allah (SWT) for guidance in making a big decision

Liabilities: The debts that a person or business owes and is obligated to pay

Margin: Borrowed money with which to invest in the stock market

Money Market: Bank product in which you deposit money and it accrues interest; similar to a savings account, but with restrictions on how much and how often you can withdraw money

Mudarabah: Method of providing funding to an entrepreneur where risk is shared between a single investor and the recipient; the investor is not involved in the management of the business

Musharakah: Method of providing funding to an entrepreneur where profit and loss are shared between multiple investors and the recipient; the investors may or may not be involved in the management of the business

Mutual Funds: A collection of stocks in various companies; creates a diversified, relatively safe investment compared to purchasing individual stocks; managed by an investment firm

Nafl: Non-obligatory, voluntary

Net Income: A company's total profits after subtracting taxes, depreciation, amortization, etc.

Net Worth: How much value one has in financial terms; it consists of one's total assets (cash, property, investments) minus total liabilities

Nisab: Minimum net worth before one is obligated to pay Zakat

Niyyah: One's intentions

Non-Fungible Token (NFT): A digital asset, like an image or audio file, that uses blockchain technology to guarantee its authenticity and uniqueness

Options: A contract that gives the buyer the right to buy or sell a security at a certain point in time at a price that is determined today

Partnership: Type of business structure where two or more people share in ownership and operation

Pension: Investment fund set up by employer for employees; regular payment is then made to them after retiring

Portfolio: One's collection of investments, such as stocks, bonds, and real estate

Principal: The amount of a loan or debt, excluding interest

Prospectus: A document detailing an investment fund's strategy, holdings, inception date, etc.

Qadr: Destiny, predetermination

Real Estate Investment Trust (REIT): Similar to a mutual fund, but based on real estate; investment company owns and operates income-producing real estate; allows average person to invest in real estate at a low cost and without the hassle of buying and managing property

Riba: Interest, usury

Rizq: Provision, sustenance, wealth

Sadaqa: Voluntary charity

Sadaqa Jariya: Ongoing charity

Salat: Ritual prayer performed by Muslims five times a day; one of the pillars of Islam

Savings Account: Bank product in which you deposit money, and the bank uses the funds to lend out to other customers, earning you interest income in return

Sawm: Fasting (i.e. during the holy month of Ramadan); one of the pillars of Islam

SAW: Acronym for *Salallahu Alayhi Wasalaam*, meaning may Allah's (SWT) peace and blessings be upon him

Securities: General term for an investment asset that can be bought and sold, including stocks and bonds

Securities and Exchange Commission (SEC): Government agency that works to ensure fair and legal trading of securities; protects investors

Shahada: Profession of faith; "there is no god but Allah, and Muhammad is His messenger"; one of the pillars of Islam

Shareholders: People who own stock in a company; technically, they have part ownership in the company

Shariah: Commonly referred to as Islamic law; rules that govern how to do things, such as how to perform the ritual prayer

Sheikh (or *Alim*): Islamic scholar; sheikh can also be used to refer to a leader or chief

Short Sale: If a homeowner is unable to make mortgage payments, he/she may work with the bank to initiate a short sale, or selling the home for less than what the mortgage balance is; the bank must agree, and the homeowner is able to get out of the mortgage; this causes a negative impact to one's credit score, but not as severe as a foreclosure

Sole Proprietorship: Type of business structure that is owned and operated by one person

Stocks: Share of ownership in a publicly traded corporation; provides capital to the company to grow/expand its business

Stock Market: Market on which shares of stock are bought and sold; examples include New York Stock Exchange (NYSE) and Nasdaq

Stock Split: When share prices get really high, companies can choose to split the stock to make the price lower; splits are typically 2-for-1 or 3-for-1; in a 2-for-1 stock split, the share price is cut in half, but existing investors now have twice as many shares

Sukuk: Islamic bond; alternative to conventional bond; technically not a debt; backed by assets

SWT: Acronym for *Subhanahu Wa Ta'ala*, meaning that all praises are for Him alone

Takaful: An Islamic form of insurance; a cooperative effort where people pool money together to protect one another against loss

Zakat: Alms; giving to help the less fortunate; calculated as 2.5% of wealth and assets; one of the pillars of Islam

www.ingramcontent.com/pod-product-compliance
Lightning Source LLC
Chambersburg PA
CBHW050008230526
45465CB00003BB/1311